Alternative Governance Structures in Megacities: Threats or Opportunities?

By

Diane E. Chido

&

U.S. Department of Defense

ISBN-13: 978-1544096827
ISBN-10: 1544096828

The United States Army War College

The United States Army War College educates and develops leaders for service at the strategic level while advancing knowledge in the global application of Landpower.

The purpose of the United States Army War College is to produce graduates who are skilled critical thinkers and complex problem solvers. Concurrently, it is our duty to the U.S. Army to also act as a "think factory" for commanders and civilian leaders at the strategic level worldwide and routinely engage in discourse and debate concerning the role of ground forces in achieving national security objectives.

The Strategic Studies Institute publishes national security and strategic research and analysis to influence policy debate and bridge the gap between military and academia.

The Center for Strategic Leadership contributes to the education of world class senior leaders, develops expert knowledge, and provides solutions to strategic Army issues affecting the national security community.

The Peacekeeping and Stability Operations Institute provides subject matter expertise, technical review, and writing expertise to agencies that develop stability operations concepts and doctrines.

The School of Strategic Landpower develops strategic leaders by providing a strong foundation of wisdom grounded in mastery of the profession of arms, and by serving as a crucible for educating future leaders in the analysis, evaluation, and refinement of professional expertise in war, strategy, operations, national security, resource management, and responsible command.

The U.S. Army Heritage and Education Center acquires, conserves, and exhibits historical materials for use to support the U.S. Army, educate an international audience, and honor Soldiers—past and present.

STRATEGIC STUDIES INSTITUTE

The Strategic Studies Institute (SSI) is part of the U.S. Army War College and is the strategic-level study agent for issues related to national security and military strategy with emphasis on geostrategic analysis.

The mission of SSI is to use independent analysis to conduct strategic studies that develop policy recommendations on:

- Strategy, planning, and policy for joint and combined employment of military forces;

- Regional strategic appraisals;

- The nature of land warfare;

- Matters affecting the Army's future;

- The concepts, philosophy, and theory of strategy; and,

- Other issues of importance to the leadership of the Army.

Studies produced by civilian and military analysts concern topics having strategic implications for the Army, the Department of Defense, and the larger national security community.

In addition to its studies, SSI publishes special reports on topics of special or immediate interest. These include edited proceedings of conferences and topically oriented roundtables, expanded trip reports, and quick-reaction responses to senior Army leaders.

The Institute provides a valuable analytical capability within the Army to address strategic and other issues in support of Army participation in national security policy formulation.

Strategic Studies Institute
and
U.S. Army War College Press

ALTERNATIVE GOVERNANCE STRUCTURES IN MEGACITIES: THREATS OR OPPORTUNITIES?

Diane E. Chido

November 2016

*****

Comments pertaining to this report are invited and should be forwarded to: Director, Strategic Studies Institute and U.S. Army War College Press, U.S. Army War College, 47 Ashburn Drive, Carlisle, PA 17013-5010.

*****

This manuscript was funded by the U.S. Army War College External Research Associates Program. Information on this program is available on our website, *www.StrategicStudies Institute.army.mil*, at the Opportunities tab.

*****

All Strategic Studies Institute (SSI) and U.S. Army War College (USAWC) Press publications may be downloaded free of charge from the SSI website. Hard copies of certain reports may also be obtained free of charge while supplies last by placing an order on the SSI website. Check the website for availability. SSI publications may be quoted or reprinted in part or in full with permission and appropriate credit given to the U.S. Army Strategic Studies Institute and U.S. Army War College Press, U.S. Army War College, Carlisle, PA. Contact SSI by visiting our website at the following address: *www.StrategicStudiesInstitute.army.mil*.

*****

The Strategic Studies Institute and U.S. Army War College Press publishes a monthly email newsletter to update the national security community on the research of our analysts, recent and forthcoming publications, and upcoming conferences sponsored by the Institute. Each newsletter also provides a strategic commentary by one of our research analysts. If you are interested in receiving this newsletter, please subscribe on the SSI website at *www.StrategicStudiesInstitute.army.mil/newsletter*.

*****

The author would like to acknowledge Kayley Morrison for her excellent research and analysis assistance, her impeccable writing, and her effective management of the author throughout the process. Any errors or omissions are entirely the author's responsibility.

ISBN 1-58487-740-5

FOREWORD

Many cities are growing into "mega" land areas filled with complex terrain and populations where the U.S. military will undoubtedly have to engage. Often, states fail to provide basic services to some territories, leaving inhabitants disenfranchised. These gaps are then filled by social entrepreneurs, often ethnic or religious-based civil society groups — or even organized crime syndicates — who effectively identify niche needs in the marketplace and fill them more effectively than other competitors, including traditional state authorities. Leaders of these groups maintain control through various means, including: violence, coercion, and service provision; or through tribal, religious, or other cultural ties and structures.

In order to understand and predict the emergence of alternative governance, and to identify whether it represents a threat or opportunity to U.S. interests, we must develop a toolkit, which can be based on existing sources and analytic methods that only need to be expanded to the city level or weighted and appropriately applied. Such foreknowledge is a force multiplier for planning and operating in an urban environment, particularly one as dense as a megacity.

DOUGLAS C. LOVELACE, JR.
Director
Strategic Studies Institute and
    U.S. Army War College Press

ABOUT THE AUTHOR

DIANE E. CHIDO is the President of DC Analytics, a research and analysis firm formed in October 2008. Since the drafting of this monograph, she has become the Security and Intelligence Advisor to the U.S. Army's Peace Keeping and Stability Operations Institute (PKSOI). She has served as a cultural awareness subject matter expert on the Horn of Africa and is assisting in creating training materials for the U.S. Army and course curricula in cultural intelligence analysis for academic and intelligence community agencies. She has also performed extensive research on Sub-Saharan African civil-military relations, socio-cultural cleavages, and regional security threats and opportunities. Ms. Chido is an adjunct instructor of intelligence studies with the Tom Ridge College of Intelligence Studies and Data Informatics at Mercyhurst University as well as a graduate of that program. She teaches intelligence communication, advanced intelligence analysis, and advanced analytic techniques, in the classroom and online at the graduate and undergraduate levels. She has also served as a faculty advisor for student researchers on nearly a dozen Department of Defense (DoD) contracts with the Center for Intelligence Research, Analysis, and Training (CIRAT). Ms. Chido has 20 years of experience in research, including with the International Monetary Fund and with the Brookings Institution Foreign Policy Program. She publishes widely on intelligence analysis, ethnic conflict, and international security topics. Ms. Chido holds an M.S. in applied intelligence analysis, an M.A. in Russian language, and a graduate certificate in Russian/East European studies.

SUMMARY

Many cities are growing into "mega" land areas filled with complex terrain and populations where the U.S. military will undoubtedly have to engage. States often fail to provide basic services to some territories, leaving inhabitants disenfranchised. These gaps are then filled by social entrepreneurs, often ethnic or religious-based civil society groups—or even organized crime syndicates—who effectively identify niche needs in the marketplace and fill them more effectively than other competitors, including traditional state authorities. Leaders of these groups maintain control through various means, including: violence, coercion, and service provision; or through tribal, religious, or other cultural ties and structures.

As the 21st century progresses, the role and structure of government is already evolving from the current Westphalian, nation-state-based system originating in the 17th century to one more loosely based on alternative governance structures (AGS), the form and function of which we are only beginning to understand. This phenomenon is easy to imagine in fragile states; however, as industrialized nations become increasingly polarized by economic inequality; as citizens' trust in the effectiveness and motives of state authorities erodes; and as social media tools help AGS organize and operate, they are also likely to become a greater threat to state authority in the developed world.

While examining AGS types, not all have a violent or profit-seeking structure. There are also civil society and faith-based organizations providing services that are the traditional responsibility of states, which can also (wittingly or otherwise) undermine its authority peacefully. This is why it is important to focus on the structures that emerge, as opposed to the individual groups themselves, to enable identification of the varying types of alternative governance arising in these immense urban areas before conflict or other circumstances erupt that the United States considers to be against its national interest.

If the state is unable to predict the emergence of such alternatives to its own influence, and always assumes that it must challenge and eradicate them, the result will be numerous small-scale violent conflicts that undermine regional and global stability and endanger energy, food, and human security. Unless states can understand the factors causing these structures to emerge and threaten their authority, they will be unprepared to determine whether it is in their interest to halt the development of these alternative governance models, or to share this market with nongovernmental or sub-state actors in order to actually maintain or enhance the state's own legitimacy.

Within existing or emerging AGS, identifying norm-based governance factors such as reputation, trust, reciprocity, enforcement of compliance, and self-regulation can be keys to the effective communication of tactical or operational goals. In addition, the introduction of respected figures that will assist in attaining goals that are of U.S. interest is a critical method of undermining coercive or other leadership whose objectives run counter to U.S. interests.

It can be difficult for outsiders to understand the complex social networks, incentives, and motivations that underlie AGS, making it nearly impossible to determine with whom to negotiate and what leverage might be effective to further U.S. goals. In addition, the amount and type of power that members or leaders of such structures wield in actuality, as opposed to assurances, is critical to gauge—especially in a climate of shifting alliances. Planning and movement are also inhibited by the poor mapping, weak infrastructure, and the disordered slums of megacities, all of which can be nearly impossible to monitor or access.

In order to understand and predict the emergence of alternative governance, and to identify whether it represents a threat or opportunity to U.S. interests, we must develop a toolkit, which can be based on existing sources and analytic methods that only need to be expanded to the city level or weighted and appropriately applied. Such foreknowledge is a force multiplier and an important nonlethal weapon for planning and operating in an urban environment, particularly one as dense as a megacity.

In addition to social network analysis methods, cultural features, such as shared dialect or language and a history of opposition to state control or of intergroup conflict, are important factors for understanding the development of AGS. More specifically, with enhanced sample sizes and updated information, measurable cultural factors can be attributed to residents of targeted megacities. These include Geert Hofstede's concepts of power distance, individualism vs. collectivism, and uncertainty avoidance.

In looking at trends in urbanization, the focus is on governance and the factors directly related to it from the average citizen's perspective; in its most basic form, this includes providing security, economic opportunity, and other basic services. To this end, a number of existing indices can be applied to provide a picture of megacities of increasing importance to U.S. defense planning, including Transparency International's Corruption Perception Index, certain elements of the U.S. Institute for Peace's Fragile States

Index, the Legatum Institute's Prosperity Index, and the United Nations (UN) Habitat Program's Cities Prosperity Index.

These measures, along with cultural dimensions and basic demographic, political, and economic data, added to critical field-based human intelligence (HUMINT) sources, can provide a set of very basic indicators for piecing together the contextual environment in which the selected megacities exist, as well as their own prosperity and growth projections. Such an expandable toolbox would be invaluable for U.S. Army planners to provide a starting point for developing critical pre-knowledge of these locales and what is governing them.

ALTERNATIVE GOVERNANCE STRUCTURES IN MEGACITIES: THREATS OR OPPORTUNITIES?

> Megacities are growing, they are becoming more connected, and the ability of host nation governments to effectively deal with their explosive growth and maintain security is, in many cases, diminishing. Megacities are a unique environment that the U.S. Army does not fully understand.[1]

INTRODUCTION

Steven Pinker reminded us in his 2011 book, *The Better Angels of our Nature,* that: "feuding among knights and peasants was not just a nuisance but a lost opportunity," eventually turning, "Warriors to courtiers."[2] The concept of modern-day "warlords" controlling urban territory, and from whom the United States with all its might could not wrest control, came into the American consciousness with a jolt in 1993 Somalia. The videos of Third World thugs attacking a modern multinational force trying to provide humanitarian assistance was a shock that Americans of that generation will not forget.

Monikers such as "warlords," "brigands," and "insurgents" connote our distaste for non-traditional power structures in far-flung cities that we believe should all be run by Rotarian-like mayors and city councils. The state of the world today belies this false sense of what constitutes "governing." Urban planners suggest that effective governing means providing the basic goods and services people need to live "normal" lives, such as clean water, food, shelter, and security. In many places, cities are growing into massive land areas filled with enormous slums where vast numbers of people are not receiving these basic goods and ser-

1

vices from their central government, if at all. In portions of these "megacities," services are not provided by traditional means, but by gangs or others who are essentially effective social entrepreneurs, identifying niche needs in the marketplace and filling them more effectively than other potential competitors, including traditional state authorities. These leaders control specific territories or populations by various means, including: violence, coercion, and service provision; or through tribal, religious, or other cultural ties and structures.

The impact of such cultural networks cannot be discounted in the role played by alternative governance structures (AGS) in megacities. In his 2013 book, *Revenge of Geography*, Robert Kaplan argues:

> It is the very impersonal quality of urban life, which is lived among strangers, that accounts for intensified religious [or other deep personal identifying] feeling. For in the village of old, religion was a natural extension of the daily traditions and routine of life among the extended family; but migrations to the city brought Arab Muslims into the anonymity of slum existence, and to keep the family together and the young from drifting into crime, religion has had to be reinvented in starker, more ideological form. In this way, states weaken, or at least have to yield somewhat, to new and sometimes extreme kinds of nationalism and religiosity advanced by urbanization.[3]

This phenomenon could also easily be seen among other immigrant populations in any megacity, such as the clichéd ubiquity of Italian and Irish adherence to Catholicism across New York City, since large waves of both groups began coming to the United States and continuing today in many communities across the country. This reinforcement of identity enabled *pae-*

sani, or Italians of a shared regional group in Italy, to eventually grow influence networks into larger economic units of Italians, rather than only segmented Sicilians, Napolitanos, or Calabrese, who initially fought turf wars against each other in American cities.

As the 21st century progresses, the role and structure of government is already evolving from the current Westphalian, nation-state-based system originating in the 17th century to one more loosely based on AGS, the form and function of which are only beginning to be understood.

As Francis Fukuyama, Phil Williams, and many others have argued, traditional governance structures are under siege. Jennifer Keister argues that misnamed:

> 'ungoverned spaces' exist and persist because the costs of incorporating them are too high, and the benefits of integrating them (and the risks of not doing so) are too low.[4]

Keister adds:

> Contrary to their popular characterizations, political order in these areas has not disappeared: it is simply wielded by actors other than the state, such as traditional or religious elites, warlords, community groups, and rebel organizations.[5]

As Williams noted in his 2008 Strategic Studies Institute (SSI) monograph, "the sooner we understand what may attempt to replace them [AGS], the better we will be able to mitigate negative effects on stability and security."[6]

This evolution will be more rapid and widespread in developing areas where people are "living on the edge," disenfranchised or beyond the reach of centralized government control and influence. However, as industrialized nations become increasingly polarized by economic inequality; as citizens' trust in the effectiveness and motives of state authorities erodes; and as social media tools help AGS organize and operate, this phenomenon is also likely to become a greater threat to state authority in the developed world.

If the state is unable to predict the emergence of such alternatives to its own influence, and always assumes that it must challenge and eradicate them, the result will be numerous small-scale violent conflicts that undermine regional and global stability, and endanger energy, food, and human security. Unless states can understand the factors causing these structures to emerge and threaten the state's authority, they will be unprepared to determine whether it is in their interest to halt the development of these alternative governance models or to share this market with non-governmental or sub-state actors in order to actually maintain or enhance the state's own legitimacy.

Identifying and defining the types of nontraditional governance structures, and understanding how, where, and why they emerge, can reduce future conflict and increase stability by signaling whether a state should challenge, cooperate with, or co-opt these structures as a means of enhancing the state's reach, effectiveness, and legitimacy. This knowledge is critical to mission success in locales that U.S. and allied land forces may need to be deployed to over the next 20 years and can serve as a strategic multiplier for the U.S. military and its policy planners by:

- Increasing the understanding of emerging areas of potential urban instability and conflict;
- Assisting defense budgetary analysis, resource allocation, and force planning;

- Facilitating conflict mitigation before violence erupts, thereby avoiding costly expenditures of both blood and treasure;
- Identifying true social, political, and economic centers of gravity among foreign populations before forces are committed to deploy in order to determine appropriate measures of mission success.

GOVERNANCE: A MATTER OF TRUST

When people do not trust the state, the door is opened for an AGS to set up operations. A review of current literature on governance and legitimacy suggests the primary common factor that ensures popular support of authority in a given geographic location is trust. This does not mean agreement with the methods of governing, but involves a belief in the consistent application of laws or expressed social mores across the territory (i.e., "truth, justice, and the American Way").

This trust can be earned through the effective provision of needed services, such as security; logistics to obtain and distribute adequate food, water, and other critical goods; dispute mediation, healthcare, and other social services; or it can be earned through consistent application of violence or other coercive measures. This concept of trust is not equivalent to Western notions of "good" governance, only an assurance that the population can plan and organize itself and its activities in a clear and predictable manner, even under threat of violence, as long as there is some consistency in its application.

It is critical to identify the specific sources of trust that impart legitimacy on AGS and their leaders, whether benevolent, coercive, or something in between, in order to understand how to co-opt, support, or undermine that trust to enhance mission success once defined. Conflict is more likely to arise when the population does not have this sense of trust, and when "laws" or social norms and mores serving in that capacity are not applied consistently resulting in chaos and uncertainty. Conflict is, of course, more likely in times of transition, whether due to economic, political, or social change; or due to natural or manmade disasters. This is the case even under more effective or benevolent governance structures, as the population is unsettled and unable to conduct its daily affairs in an atmosphere of certainty.

Examples of unexpected governance structures effectively creating a sense of trust abound. This would include the coercive government of Tito's Yugoslavia, until the fall of the Soviet Union triggered an economic disruption that ended the relative economic prosperity and peaceful cohabitation of nearly a dozen ethnic groups and resulted in chaos and dissolution with well-documented catastrophic results.

Aside from such state examples, unexpected governance structures also appeared in the housing projects of Chicago, a few blocks from the esteemed university. Sudhir Venkatesh vividly describes in his 2008 book, *Gang Leader for a Day*, how a Black Kings midlevel gang leader effectively governed a society apart from and forgotten by the city surrounding it, ensuring relative stability, security, and economic benefits for the poor residents of a slum slated for demolition. Pinker notes that such structures arise due to: "Mistrust of the criminal justice system turned into cynicism and sometimes paranoia, making self-help justice seem the only alternative."[7]

The Taliban even initially gave parts of southern Afghanistan a break from the chaos of the civil war resulting from three primary "warlords" vying for dominance for 2 decades. As a junior researcher at the Brookings Institution in 1994, amid the outcry against the Taliban's brutality as it roared across Afghanistan, the author recalls a small article in the *The Washington Post* noting that the vanguard of warriors were soon followed by convoys of trucks bearing food and other goods that people had in short supply, and thinking: "These guys are brilliant and they will be hard to get rid of."

Some observers have argued that the mistake the United Nations (UN) made in Somalia was in not engaging the local "warlords" in the process of distributing aid, thus recognizing that they were more legitimate sources of power and influence in areas of Mogadishu than the central government that had fallen 2 years earlier. Others have suggested that geography precludes some locales from being effectively governed by a central authority, and that a clan structure or chains of linked commercial centers are able to provide services and stability for larger numbers of citizens.

Understanding how AGS arise, operate, and can be co-opted or co-operated with — not just prevented and eradicated — will be an important part of strategic planning for dealing with growing threats in urban areas in the developing world, just as some U.S. cities try to do at a lower-level with community-led policing and jobs programs.

There are common characteristics shared by AGS that successfully challenge state authority, such as the services they provide, their structures, their modes of communication (including propaganda and messaging), and their relationships with residents.

Like corporations and other organizations, criminal gangs typically have a four-level hierarchical structure. The youngest, newest, and strongest members act as the armed front on the streets, whether they are directly selling drugs, collecting extortion money, or fighting armed battles for turf or other objectives. The next level is the middle managers — as in a corporation, the business end of the entity — who lead and organize the first level in daily and tactical matters. The third level is the decision-making circle, normally a council of those who have been with the group for a longer period and have risen through the ranks. These members oversee operational functions and assist the top echelon leader or leaders in developing strategies and making other significant decisions.

Like any business, the managers and third-tier "advisory board" meet on a regular basis in a pre-ordained place to plan and share information. Black Kings manager, "J.T.," surprised researcher Venkhatesh when he invited Venkhatesh to the daily "staff meeting" conducted in a Chicago diner at 7:30 each morning.[8] The specific activities of such groups on a daily and longer-term basis, as well as the amount of freedom to work independently or be innovative, depends upon the group's alignment and objectives, (whether profit-based or ideological), and the leadership style at the higher levels.

A critical difference in identifying alternative governance types is to determine whether the structure is primarily in place for capitalist profit-motivated purposes or to meet ideological goals. It is generally easier to define engagement strategies with leaders of profit-motivated AGS, who are pragmatic and forward thinking in terms of expanding profitable opportunities and limiting risks, than with fanatical ideologues who are far more focused on radically altering the current status quo instead of building a stable future for adherents.

Provision of Services.

Aside from ensuring the availability of sufficient resources and maintaining critical trade relationships and routes, the primary service guaranteed by a stable state is security. If citizens do not perceive that the state function responsible is adequately providing this key service, whether it be the military in terms of national security or municipal policing, alternative groups will fill the vacuum and ensure that security is restored, but perhaps not in a way the state would prefer. At the municipal level, such structures can take the form of neighborhood watch groups, which range from a network of alert citizens to collectively hiring private security, to armed citizens actively patrolling and often behaving as vigilantes.

In May 2014, on the highways surrounding Moscow, gunmen called the Grand Theft Auto (GTA) Gang started putting spikes on desolate stretches of roadway; when drivers stopped to check the damage to their cars, they were shot dead without even being robbed. Despite joint efforts of local police and even the Federal Security Service, in September 2014, after 14 people had been killed in this way, a drag racing group called *"Smotra"* began a vigilante crusade to stop these killings and make Moscow's highways once again safe for drivers. *Smotra* representatives spoke of participating in this dangerous mission for their family and the country, larger ideologies than revenge or simple security.

These vigilantes wore body armor, drove expensive sports cars, and about 1 in 10 was licensed to carry a firearm. They used their sports cars as bait and patrolled these areas; but then they began to stop motorists and search cars, interrogating and frightening drivers about the dangers on the roads, which disconcerted some residents who might otherwise have appreciated the group's efforts.[9]

This is an example of a group that formed (like that of a "posse" in the Wild West of the United States) for a specific purpose: to catch a criminal or group of outlaws, and typically disband once the target or threat was eliminated. Before the appearance of GTA, *Smotra* was a group of fast car aficionados, who likely disturbed the peace with their activities, but were not a criminal gang organized for profit or intent on becoming an alternative to state governance. Unless some motive becomes more attractive to *Smotra* leaders, profit for example, the group is likely to retire from vigilantism and go back to scaring motorists with their fast driving alone once this threat has passed.

However, the majority of gangs in Moscow are ethnically-based, either Russian neo-Nazis or Central Asian or Southern Russian Muslim groups, such as Chechens. These groups have historical animosity toward the state. They feel alienated on the one hand by intolerant immigration policies, and on the other by disenfranchisement by the Russian population and a legal and economic system that displays bias against them. In 2014, Russian investigators identified 883 ethnic gangs across the country, mainly comprised of small groups of legal immigrants, who perpetrate muggings and small-scale violent acts.[10]

Chief of Moscow police criminal investigative division Major General Igor Zinoviev noted in November 2014 that:

> The so-called complex of a mercenary operating on a foreign ground is characteristic of them: they have no moral limitations, and elders or clerics whom they

traditionally listen to in their home countries and who can help reach out to them are not around.[11]

This phenomenon of social limiters on the behavior of young men is well presented by William Reno in his chapter in *Ungoverned Spaces* regarding challenges for al-Qaeda recruitment in Somalia:

> As young supporters arrived from other parts of the country, they shed the social strictures that governed their behavior in their home communities. . . . [t]hus young men . . . would be more willing to use violence on behalf of their patrons with assurance they would not suffer the usual social consequences.[12]

In the case of megacities, many young people moving to cities, ostensibly to find economic opportunities to support their families and home communities, can be drawn into criminal, ideological, or other forms of AGS as they find themselves in a new environment with lessened family and community involvement, even if they share their new urban space with members of their ethnic group or clan. Absent the imposition of traditional community mores, these "displaced" urbanites can become highly effective AGS members subverting state authority, as they are more willing to commit acts that would be negatively perceived or prohibited by religious or other moral codes enforced more easily by local religious or family leaders in the home community.

In order for the U.S. military to effectively operate as needed in megacities, these structures must be understood in terms of: the source of trust; the level and type of services they provide; and the networks among them, in order to plan and seek allies and opportunities for cooperation with or the undermining of one group by supporting another. However, as was done in order to counter the Soviet aggression in Afghanistan in the 1980s, support of the *mujahidin* (holy warriors of God) engendered a greater threat for the future. Longer-term studies of such structures and longer-term post-conflict relationship-building activities are required as AGS goals and opportunities change.

Trust and Culture.

Within existing or emerging AGS, identifying norm-based governance factors such as reputation, trust, reciprocity, enforcement of compliance, and self-regulation can be keys to the effective communication of tactical or operational goals. In addition, the introduction of respected figures that will assist in attaining goals that are of U.S. interest is a critical method of undermining coercive or other leadership styles whose objectives run counter to U.S. interests.

It can be difficult for outsiders to understand the complex social networks, incentives, and motivations that underlie AGS, making it nearly impossible to determine with whom to negotiate and what leverage might be effective to further U.S. goals. In addition, the amount and type of power that members or leaders of such structures wield in actuality, as opposed to assurances, is critical to gauge — especially in a climate of shifting alliances. Planning and movement are also inhibited by the poor mapping, weak infrastructure, and disordered slums of megacities, all of which can be nearly impossible to monitor or access.[13]

Community Attitudes.

Community attitudes toward crime, fault, punishment, and justice also affect the creation and maintenance of AGS. Identifying how a given AGS runs counter to these attitudes can provide an opening to undermining or gradually changing how these structures evolve. Typically, AGS arise in times of transition, when uncertainty and instability are increasing. Even coercive AGS can provide a sense of security and normalcy that most residents prefer over chaos.

In many places, as political "progress" takes place in directions seen as positive in the West, new laws may run counter to long-held mores, such as loyalty to one's ethnic group or tribe, family, religion, or region. This sense of obligation can cause persons in both the public and the private sectors to go against the law without concern or an internal sense of operating unethically.[14]

Expression of Shared Values: Method and Messaging.

Even now in a time of advanced telecommunications, with Islamic terrorist groups effectively using social media to communicate and recruit members with increasingly sophisticated messaging and videography, all forms of AGS communication must be understood. As the pony express and the telegraph made their way across the newly colonized western United States, Native Americans continued to thwart modern communication methods with traditional smoke signals and drum beats.

By the same token, post-9/11, the United States was highly successful in disrupting significant financial networks involving witting or unwitting Islamic charities funding terrorist activities. However, more difficult to track cash transactions, *hawala* (transfer) trust networks, or chains of bartered services must be taken into account when defining AGS activities and methods of financial transaction for U.S. entities to attempt to disrupt or insinuate themselves into them for operational or strategic purposes.

Aside from identifying communication networks within AGS in megacities, the content of the messaging is crucial to understand. Current effective terrorist propaganda has become far more sophisticated than the proletariat slogans and icons that now seem laughable in the Soviet period. On a special segment of CNN's *Global Public Square* on the Islamic State in Iraq and the Levant (ISIL) that aired in July 2015, host Fareed Zakaria noted:

> a lot of the propaganda mixes the violence with scenes of camaraderie, friendship. The people in ISIS [sic] videos seem to be saying, 'We did not belong where we were but now we have found a home,' a powerful message to the millions of unemployed, disconnected, young Muslims across the Middle East and even in countries like France and Germany.[15]

Appearing on the same episode, Jürgen Todenhöfer, a German journalist who spent time in ISIL-controlled Mosul reported:

> The amazing thing is that they [ISIL recruits] are completely enthusiastic. They think it's the time of their life. They think that they are part of a historical event changing the whole Middle East. . . . There are even recruitment videos for deaf jihadists who wish to join.[16]

Dimensions of Culture as a Predictive Model.

Cultural features, such as shared dialect or language, or a history of opposition to state control or of inter-group conflict, are important factors contributing to the creation and maintenance of AGS. More specifically, with enhanced sample sizes and updated information, measurable cultural factors can be attributed to residents of targeted megacities, such as those developed by Geert Hofstede, including power distance, individualism vs. collectivism, and uncertainty avoidance. Figure 1 below compares three of Hofstede's Dimensions of National Culture in four widely divergent countries containing megacities to be explored further: the United States (New York City) as a baseline only, Russia (Moscow), Pakistan (Karachi), and Nigeria (Lagos).

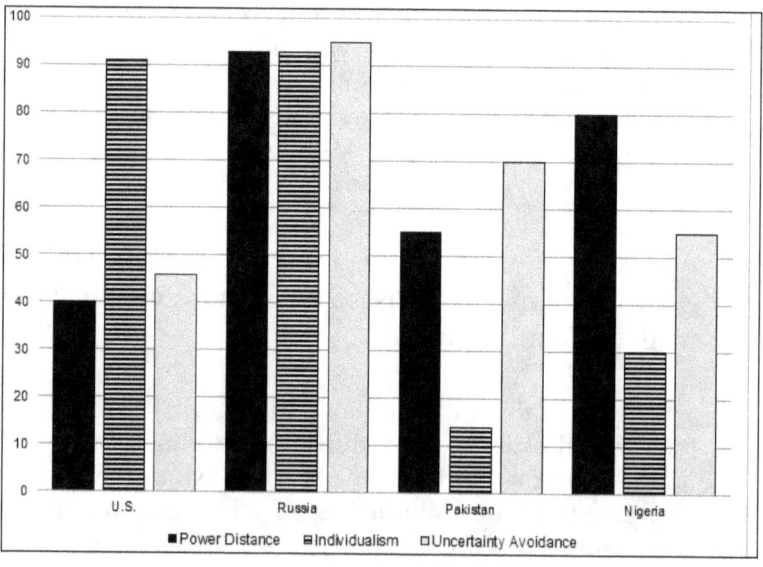

Figure 1. Comparison of Hofsteade's Dimension of National Culture.

Power Distance: According to Hofstede, power distance refers to "the extent to which the less powerful members of institutions and organizations within a country expect and accept that power is distributed unequally."[17] High power-distance countries tend to operate within a vassal system, such as that prevalent in Medieval Europe in which subordinates are dependent for protection or economic or political gain from superiors.[18]

In such cases, favors are exchanged for loyalty, a process that can continue for generations in a paternalistic bond difficult to quantify from the outside but fully understood by the participants. Such a system engenders corruption from a Western perspective that actually provides a level of stability and certainty until some transitional period when the strength of the superior is diminished or the subordinate has the opportunity and motive to subvert the system.

Such transition can take place suddenly due to a reversal of fortune resulting from a catastrophic event or through a gradual, strategic process as took place in Europe at the creation of the Westphalian State. Knights marauding across the countryside, like modern-day "warlords" or today's battles for drug turf, were economically detrimental to increasingly powerful European kings as villages were destroyed, arable land burned, and peasants killed, thus reducing the given region's overall productivity and economic return.

The trick was to entice or coerce a knight to defer the right to use violence toward the state, for a larger "national" defense was difficult because it could appear weak to other knights or lesser nobles. This required the state to be vigilant in administering violence in a measured and consistent capacity in order to keep peace and discourage a resumption of revenge killings and attacks for plunder. The head of state had to ensure that his power was sufficient, to ensure that currying his favor was more attractive than subverting it. Pinker calls this process of creating the "Leviathan," the turning of "warriors into courtiers," one of the most significant developments in the stabilizing and civilizing process.[19] If the state is unable to maintain this appearance of supreme power, members of high-power distance cultures can dissolve into AGS based on paternalism.

High-power distance cultures can also tolerate far greater degrees of inequality than lower-power distance cultures, so unfair distribution of economic opportunity is considered a fact of life and not imperative to strive to overcome for oneself or for the greater good.

As illustrated in Figure 1, if we apply this cultural dimension to four megacity host countries, it is clear that as the United States has low power distance at 40, it is not surprising that rising inequality has become a significant political issue that the populace feels empowered to act to reverse. Pakistan has a relatively neutral power distance level at 55, which Hofstede suggests is inconclusive. Nigeria is much higher at 80, suggesting that people in that country tend to expect a lot from the state in terms of services and subsidies, and they are likely to turn to other sources of governance in their absence. Russia demonstrates a very high power distance level at 93, which is not surprising considering the centuries-long imperial serf system that eventually reinvented itself as the Communist Party hierarchy and others, indicating democratization will likely take a long time and will need a different sort of ruling class to emerge in Russia. While a severe economic disruption always has the chance of creating conflict, cultures with high power distance are also likely to be more tolerant of poor national economic performance that affects the lower classes.

Individualism vs. Collectivism: This cultural factor relates to the extent to which an individual expects life decisions and directions to be determined by the individual himself or the group to which he belongs; whether that is defined as the family, nuclear or far extended; friends or peers; or religious or ethnic groups.

Expecting democratic values and individual choice to be primary in collectivist cultures is a nonstarter for peacekeeping and civil society. Coercive AGS can be highly effective in collectivist cultures such as Pakistan, which ties with China for a score of 14 (not shown), as group harmony is seen as more important than individual rights, even when maintaining the peace can cause great harm to a significant number of individuals. This was evident when Chinese civil society groups attempted to co-opt power from the Chinese state in the 1980s, resulting in the events at Tiananmen Square in 1989. From the perspective of an American college student in China at the time, CIA Analyst Dr. Rob Johnston recalls:

> It seemed inconceivable that the citizens of Beijing — 10-12 million people — would not intervene on behalf of the students. That many people could have overwhelmed the PLA [Peoples' Liberation Army] had they chosen to do so. I also assumed that the soldiers of the PLA would be reluctant to fire on their own people, partly because the majority of both groups were from the same, dominant ethnic group of China, the Han, and, in part, because the soldiers represented a lower rung of Chinese society then did the students . . . I was wrong.[20]

In hindsight, Johnston recognized that:

> In China, the protesting students were seen as a direct challenge to political authority and . . . their actions were viewed as an outright conflict between the future elite and the current leadership. The protest itself was viewed as a violation of a taboo, upsetting the cultural order and the stability of society.[21]

This view is borne out with China's low individualist score of 20 (not shown), which is not surprising given the historical emphasis placed on the harmony of the group, as illustrated by Dr. Johnston's experience in 1989.

The United States defines itself as a country of "rugged individuals," so a high score of 93 is not surprising, but Russia shares the same score, despite the high power distance and its collectivist political history. Pakistan's highly collectivist score of 14 indicates that loyalty to the group (whether it is the family, or an ethnic or religious group) trumps merit, which affects everything from commercial and employment practices to political elections, leading to a high tolerance of Western-defined corruption easily manifesting itself in the official and unofficial governance structures in a megacity like Karachi. Nigeria is a bit more individualistic than Pakistan, but is still far more collectivist than the United States or Russia with a score of 30, again contributing to a "tribal" political climate and widespread corruption.

Uncertainty Avoidance: This cultural factor reflects intolerance for ambiguity within a given culture, often leading to strong traditional beliefs and adherence to rules in order to attempt to control daily consistency for familiar outcomes, even if the rules are actually detrimental to the individual's progress and well-being. In such cultures, Western perceptions of corrupt systems, even at the state level, can be viewed as a mechanism to reduce uncertainty. In situations where outcomes are uncertain, corruption may serve to secure a more certain result. For example, M.S. Alam describes how government officials in passport offices in uncertainty avoidant cultures "create the potential for illicit gains by causing delays and uncertainty in the processing of applications."[22] Salim Rashid observed that providing an appropriate bribe while contracting for utility services reduces uncertainty and increases efficiency in some third-world countries.[23]

Always a culture of extremes, Russia is the highest uncertainty avoiding culture with a score of 95, which helps to explain how the imperial and communist regimes were able to maintain control of the population for so long with coercive yet predicable policies, and through an ideological fervor that equated the tsar with God and tied the Party to every individual. Pakistan is the next intolerant of uncertainty at 70, which helps explain the lean toward the traditional practice of Islam and the development of deep pockets of religious extremism.

Nigeria and the United States are rather moderate at 55 and 46 respectively; this suggests a greater openness to innovation and a lower need for lots of rules. To this end, a Nigerian doctor living and working in the United States recently commented to the author: "Lagos is total chaos. Things have gotten a lot better in the past decade but those people have lived with chaos forever, they don't know how to function without it."[24] Despite its collectivist preference for harmony, Chinese culture has a high tolerance for uncertainty. This is likely influenced by the Confucian worldview that suggests the world and its history operate on a system of recurring cycles that cannot be controlled but are also generally predictable.

Although the Western press is rife with examples of the horror and disruption caused by the march of ISIL across the Levant, rather than only destroying cities in its path, in some cases it has become an almost welcome AGS. Fareed Zakaria reported that in Mosul (a city in Iraq with a score of 85 for uncertainty avoidance), ISIL actually provides a level of security that has been absent in Iraq since the U.S. invasion, even with ISIL-branded police cars and officers issuing traffic tickets. Mosul residents told journalist Todenhöfer that under Iraq's Shiite government they suffered from the chaos and are now better off under ISIL. Todenhöfer noted, "instead of anarchy they have now law and order. And people don't like [ISIL] but they like their security. So they take taxes. They take care of the poor."[25] In the same segment, Zakaria opined, "while there is an allure to security in the abstract, no one likes living under a brutal theocracy." This juxtaposition of perception and fact is the key to determining whether and how to counter or co-opt AGS.[26]

Unfortunately, Hofstede's model is only a starting point for this type of cultural analysis, because it was last updated in 2010, thereby extending his original research conducted between 1967 and 1973 with a too-small sample of participants from 76 countries. Updating his results and weighting the key cultural dimensions outlined here, however, would result in scores that could determine which select cultures are more or less susceptible to the development of viable AGS that could threaten the sovereignty of the state.

Using the current data and weighting all three attributes equally, as noted in Table 1, Russia has the high score of 94, and in 1917, an alternative governance model developed by Vladimir Lenin did topple the existing state and create a new governing architecture for the entire Russian Empire.

Countries	United States	Russia	Pakistan	Nigeria
Power Distance	40	93	55	80
Individualism	91	93	14	30
Uncertainty Avoidance	46	95	70	55
Average Score on 3 Dimensions	59	95	46	55

Table 1. Comparison of Select Dimensions of National Culture.

The remaining cultures are moderates, but the argument can be made that the next high scorer is the United States. Although U.S. sovereignty and stability are believed to be secure, there are thousands of AGS that co-opt the state's monopoly on power; and yet they exist without interference from and often working with the blessing of the state. These include trade unions, civil society organizations, and even Amish or closed Mormon communities, all of whom provide services to their constituents, often persuade their members how to participate (or not) in the political process, and do not contribute to the public purse.

Nigeria is the next high scorer at 55, although moderately so. From 1966, Nigeria experienced a series of *coups d'état* by various uncoordinated military leaders; but this is in no way similar to the complete societal change wrought by the Communist Party in Russia, which had erected its own governance structures underground during the empire period. These coups were a manifestation of the weakness of state institutions, which can still describe much of the

Nigerian government today, making it too politically weak to effectively manage any AGS that may emerge. This series of military coups could suggest that Nigeria's military itself was an AGS, only ostensibly under state control; however, the vicious and violent competition for the top position in the Nigerian government indicated personal ambition and sectoral infighting within the military, prohibiting any form of governance that might have become a viable alternative to a Westphalian state model.

The lowest scorer, Pakistan (46) is again at the median, which does not provide a clear indication of the cultural threshold for any developing AGS that could threaten state control. Pakistan's score is mainly a combination of very low levels of individualism and tolerance for uncertainty, which suggest that existing tribal and family structures, along with strong religious beliefs and Muslim or local mores, already govern individual Pakistanis more than does the central government. In that case, AGS emerging in Karachi — aided by the forces of urbanization and modernity that draw those in megacities to seek structures to provide the safety of a collective and enhance certainty — are likely to lend themselves to a cultural disposition to being governed locally by a trusted AGS, but disregard the central government. Pakistan's mountainous geography already drives a cultural apathy to the central government in preference to regional interests; much like the U.S. Federal structure, which gives significant power to individual states and shared regional interests.

WHY FOCUS ON MEGACITIES?

Recent U.S. Chair of the Joint Chiefs General Raymond Odierno explained the importance of studying megacities in his introduction to his Strategic Studies Group's 2014 report, *Megacities and the United States Army: Preparing for a Complex and Uncertain Future*, by stating:

> increasing urbanization throughout the world is making the megacity one of the key features of many potential operational theaters . . . most of the world's population will be in urban areas . . . a problem that we must begin to understand and for which we must prepare.[27]

General Odierno also pointed out that: "our Army has experience throughout its history of operating in urban environments. . . . [w]e have not, however, operated in urban areas with populations over 10 million people."[28] In addition, the report notes that missions are centered around actions to influence people, which perfectly aligns with the idea of understanding the governance structures that are operating or evolving within megacities to a degree that we can identify non-military influence opportunities.

General Odierno's own team asks rhetorically and responds:

> Why would the U.S. Army go to one of these places? . . . [u]nderlying that question is an understanding that current Army doctrine and historic military judgment advocates avoiding urban areas in general for reasons of practicality and risk.[29]

Counterinsurgency expert David Kilcullen argues that violent nonstate actors (VNSAs) will increasingly focus on the urban environments of the world's emerging megacities, and the Naval War College's Richard J. Norton warns that "feral" cities provide breeding grounds for criminal and terrorist networks. In response, the Department of Defense (DoD) has turned to developing doctrine and operations appropriate to these spaces. Central governments have limited presence and control in places "as varied as" Pakistan's Federally Administered Tribal Areas, northern Yemen, and the slum areas of megacities such as Rio de Janeiro and Karachi.[30]

It is easy to focus on VNSAs when considering alternative governance in megacities as we typically hear more about groups that are expanding influence through violence with states' inability to halt their progress, such as Boko Haram in Nigeria or ISIL. In addition to ideological violent groups, there are also intra- and interstate criminal networks, such as drug cartels in Latin and South America and other trafficking groups as well as violent gangs, whose influence is checked by the "turf" they control within a single section of a city.

While there is interrelation between AGS and VNSAs, there is a critical distinction between the study of each. Though the VNSAs may be the individuals or groups who establish and maintain AGS, not all nonstate actors, especially VNSAs, actually govern. In fact, many insurgent or terrorist groups, such as al-Qaeda in Sudan or Somalia, may only be based in a given territory and operate entirely separate of it, focused on their own targets located elsewhere.

While examining AGS types, not all have a violent or profit-seeking structure. There are also civil society and faith-based organizations providing services that are the traditional responsibility of states, which can also (wittingly or otherwise) undermine its authority peacefully. This is why it is important to focus on the structures that emerge, as opposed to the individual groups themselves, to enable identification of the varying types of alternative governance arising in these immense urban areas before conflict or other circumstances erupt that the United States considers to be against its national interest.

Effects of Mega-Urbanization on Governance.

The movement of the world's population from increasingly rural to urban is well documented, and branches of study of the force and consequences of urbanization emerge almost daily on diverse topics in many disciplines, from environmental sustainability to infrastructure development and resource allocation.

The subject of governance develops as "megacities" emerge, and concern rises over alternatives to sovereign national units that engender localized allegiances or affiliations that become stronger than the national identity. Imagine if the U.S. Federal or even New York state structures failed so utterly to provide rescue, remediation, rebuilding, security, infrastructure, and basic services that 15 years later, by 2016, inhabitants of the megacity that is the American commercial center began operating as if they were New Yorkers first and no longer identified themselves as Americans. What would be the specific failures of state structures at all levels that might cause that outcome?

"Wild Forces," Transition and Instability.

Pinker describes a number of forces he terms "wild" that result in societies becoming more violent and unstable,[31] whereby they contribute to the creation of Williams' "dangerous spaces" where AGS are likely to emerge.[32] These include rootless or idle young men, and tribal and traditional cultures based on honor, not reason and empathy, as well as a reliance on self-help justice or a law-on-the-street honor code. Pinker adds that every human society is faced with a conflict of interest between the younger men who seek dominance (and ultimately mating opportunities) for themselves, and the older men who seek to minimize internecine damage within their extended families and clans.[33]

This phenomenon is beginning to become significant in China with the prevalence of single young men as a result of the One Child policy, which has created a severe gender gap; single young men without the civilizing influence of wives and children are likely to pose an increasing threat to the state in both rural and urban areas.

Traditional societies, such as the Igbo of Nigeria, have developed the age-mate system in which young people born in the same year are encouraged to form a supporting clique, solving disputes and assisting one another throughout their lives. Age-mate groups pride themselves on activities that enhance village life or build economic opportunity for the entire community, which engenders pride within each group that can prevent young male members from creating havoc. Movement away from these groups into larger city environments is one of the trends that can remove their desire to follow village mores; this, coupled with decreased economic opportunity, can prevent them from becoming good marriage candidates, and groups of such young men joining together can increase violence and instability.

As was noted in the section on dimensions of national culture, there are other cultural attributes that arise from traditional necessity, such as membership in a culture of honor often resulting in traditional herding communities, for instance, that can be a predictor of violence and instability within society. A prime example of this is the Hatfields and McCoys, Scottish families that settled in the mountainous area of West Virginia and Kentucky in the United States.

Their famous feud was fueled by this culture of honor common among peoples living in hilly or mountainous regions with little arable land for cultivation but well-suited for animal husbandry. If your source of wealth and status is able to wander off or be stolen, unlike something immovable such as land, you must be prepared to guard it without question. In such cultures, having a hair trigger temperament and flaring the threat of violence at any perceived slight is critical to maintaining a reputation of not being the herder to be trifled with.

Hilly or mountainous terrain also lends itself to AGS creation as such areas naturally develop independent, self-reliant communities in the "hollers" or valley areas with natural defense lines. This terrain leads to a decreased reliance upon and increased mistrust of any centralized government, especially if it means cooperating with long-time enemies in the adjoining valley with whom you have traditionally vied for resources. This is a critical issue in mountainous regions like Pakistan.

Self-help or street justice is for alienated people, whom Pinker calls "stateless," even if they are full citizens of the state in which they reside. Due to their minority status, no matter what proportion of the population they comprise, their class, race, and economic status causes them to be less or totally unprotected by the legal code that applies to the rest of the citizenry. The effectiveness of both a "legitimate" justice system and street justice are dependent upon credibility. This form of justice outside the state is a notable attribute of the code of honor described above.

Another factor affecting the loss of traditional mores that affects people moving into cities for the first time is modernity itself. This can erode traditional values centered around the family, tribe, religion, and shared traditions, which, once individuals are removed from the cradle of these forces, can be gradually replaced by "individualism, cosmopolitanism, reason and science," Pinker relates.[34] These transitional periods for individuals, communities, and states are likely to be when violence is most prevalent as social forces are realigned.

Measuring Governance in Megacities.

In looking at trends in urbanization, the focus is on governance and the factors directly related to it from the average citizen's perspective; in its most basic form, this includes providing economic opportunity, security, and other basic services.

To this end, a number of existing indices can be applied to provide a picture of megacities of increasing importance to U.S. defense planning. A basic application here includes: Lagos, Nigeria, because it is the commercial capital and the port city through which the United States imported $11.6 billion in oil in 2013;[35] and Karachi, Pakistan, due to its location at the crossroad of India and China and its state's contemporary contribution to instability in Central Asia. These are compared to two cities in two very different developed countries to identify what non-economic factors contribute to the development of alternative governance: New York City in the United States, and Moscow in the Russian Federation.

These measures, along with cultural dimensions and basic demographic, political, and economic data, added to critical field-based human intelligence (HUMINT) sources, can provide a set of very basic indicators for piecing together the contextual environment in which the selected megacities exist as well as their own prosperity and growth projections. Such an expandable toolbox is intended for U.S. Army planners to provide merely a starting point for developing critical pre-knowledge of these locales and what is governing them. These indices or their sub-elements and many other data sources, including pre-positioned reliable HUMINT collectors, must be combined and tested to determine what are the key conditions of life and how they are set and manipulated within megacities and their states to develop an early measure of alternative governance vulnerability, and to develop a lens to identify which should be eliminated and which have prospects for enhancing U.S. interests, before or during times of conflict.

The **Corruption Perceptions Index**[36] produced annually by Transparency International is a familiar governance indicator that shows how much citizens trust their leaders to operate ethically; such trust is crucial to maintaining popular support of the state as a primary governing body. Its results for 2015 indicate that, while improving, the other three cases exhibit very high levels of corruption compared to the United States, as shown in Figure 2.

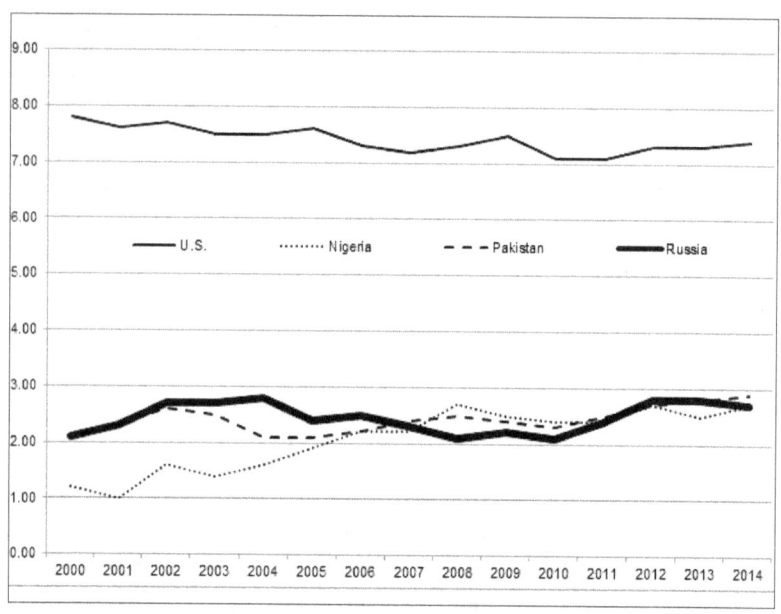

**Figure 2. Corruption Perceptions Index
Comparison, 2000-2014.**

The **Fragile States Index**, until 2013 called the "Failed States Index," produced by the U.S. Institute for Peace and *Foreign Policy Magazine* since 2005, has become a ubiquitous and valuable measure that can be easily deconstructed and its sub-elements applied to myriad challenges.[37] Those most likely to be relevant to the study of the rise of AGS include at least the following and can be carefully weighted to determine how each contributes to the emergence of AGS. They are described as such by the Fragile States Index:

- Vengeance-Seeking Group Grievance—When tension and violence exists between groups, the state's ability to provide security is undermined and fear and further violence may ensue.

- Legitimacy of the State—Corruption and a lack of representativeness in the government directly undermines the social contract.
- Progressive Deterioration of State Services—The provision of health, education, and sanitation services, among others, are key roles of the state.
- Violation of Human Rights and Rule of Law—When human rights are violated or unevenly protected, the state is failing in its ultimate responsibility.
- Security Apparatus—The security apparatus should have a monopoly on the use of legitimate force. The social contract is weakened where this is affected by competing groups.
- Rise of Factionalized Elites—When local and national leaders engage in deadlock and brinksmanship for political gain, this undermines the social contract.

The **Prosperity Index** is an annual ranking of 142 countries by the Legatum Institute, a London-based policy think tank and educational charity focused on promoting prosperity; its index is based on measurements of both income and well-being, defined by factors indicating wealth, economic growth, and quality of life. The most relevant of five sub-indicators to this study are prosperity, governance, safety, and security. As these factors are quantified using a combination of statistical indicators and qualitative information such as surveys, they take into account both economic and scientific elements as well as the perspectives of the people living within the given conditions. Figure 3 indicates lower levels of safety and security than governance in Nigeria and Pakistan, suggesting those states may have little time to enhance security provisions before they lose the remaining trust in the current government.

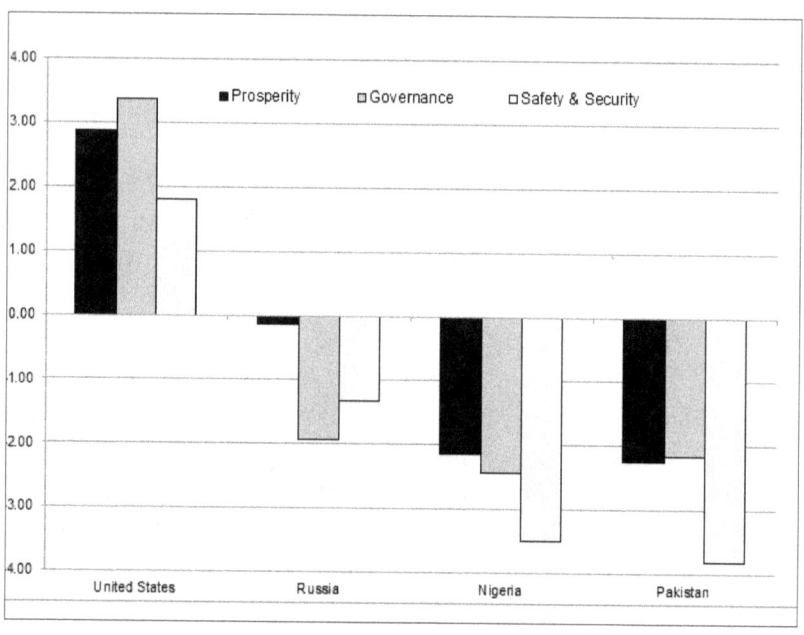

Figure 3. Legatum Prosperity Index Selected Factors, 2014.

The key study related to cities is the **Cities Prosperity Index** developed by the UN Habitat Program, which aggregates five factors: productivity, quality of life, infrastructure development, environmental sustainability, and equity and social inclusion for an overall prosperity score with 0.900 and above indicating cities with very solid prosperity factors. The latest data available is from 2012-13, and the scores for that period, unfortunately, do not include Karachi. This source also provides growth projections valuable for projecting social change, as displayed in Figure 4.

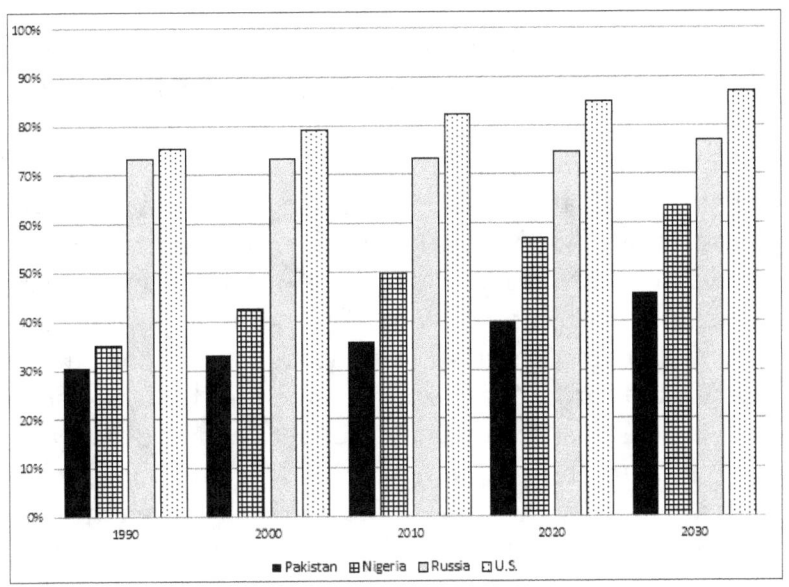

Figure 4. Rate of Urbanization Projected Through 2020.

MEGACITY CASES: KARACHI AND LAGOS

Karachi, Pakistan.

Karachi is Pakistan's only metropolitan city,[38] and is broken down into five regions. Karachi is home to more than 23.5 million people, covers 3,500 square kilometers, and has the highest literacy rates in the country, up to 90 percent in the city center.[39]

Corruption and violence have become hallmarks of Karachi's reputation. The Pakistan National Accountability Bureau has begun addressing corruption by prosecuting "mega corruption" cases against national political figures, while rampant corruption remains at lower-levels in government departments and public offices.[40]

Armed groups often use violence in Karachi as a negotiating tactic to sway provincial and federal decision-making, which can threaten the viability of the ruling coalition government. The armed wings of the major political parties, including Muttahida Quami Movement (MQM), Pakistan Peoples' Party (PPP), and Awami National Party (ANP), are the main perpetrators of urban violence. The political parties and their armed wings clash over city resources and funds generated through extortion. Karachi's ethno-political violence is based on the conflict between Urdu-speaking *mohajirs* (migrants) of the MQM against Pashtuns represented by the ANP.[41] The border between the *mohajirs* and Pashtun areas is a likely area to host ethnically based AGS emergence under this militia activity.

Violence overall has increased significantly in Karachi since 2003. Called Karachi's "bloodiest year," 2013 saw 2,700 murders.[42] This high level of crime in Karachi is not a simple phenomenon. Massive unregistered arms markets coupled with poverty and inequality have driven ethnic, political, and economic feuds to increasing violence.[43]

Karachi exemplifies a city wrought by proxy warfare in what has been called the "New Great Game," characterized by an intricate web of alliances and groups at the global, regional, and local levels that result in this spike in the murder rate. The lack of effective policing, mainly due to corruption and preferential police hiring of certain ethnic groups over others, has led to the creation of many small militias, which either protect a given group or target another.[44]

Since its official ouster from Afghanistan, the Taliban has been steadily expanding its presence in Karachi. Known domestically as Tehreek-e-Taliban Pakistan (TTP), the TTP has focused on attacking city police. Militants have gunned down police officers, assaulted police stations, and sent suicide bombers to assassinate top police commanders.[45]

Militants of many groups, including TTP, control parts of Karachi, including Sohrab Goth, Manghopir, and Ittehad Town. Over the years, TTP has made increasingly violent attacks, including one on the Sohrab Goth police station on January 29, 2013. Station House Officer Ashfaq Baloch of the Manghopir police station stated that it is difficult to impose the law in his jurisdiction and that standard operating procedures followed by law enforcement elsewhere in the city have to be modified. For instance, elsewhere in Karachi, a single officer usually responds to the scene of a killing. However, in Manghopir, law enforcement often waits for bodies to turn up in the hospitals because it is too dangerous to go to the crime scene.[46]

Karachi law enforcement has devised a map of situational no-go areas due to ethnic violence and the presence of militants and gangsters, which Karachi law enforcement does not enter under any circumstances;[47] only the paramilitary Pakistan Rangers serve as these sectors' security presence.[48] Other areas on the map are no-go areas only for a particular ethnicity in times of ethnic violence.[49] Municipal law enforcement does maintain a presence in less tense areas.[50] The prevalence of violence in ethnically segregated neighborhoods has made Karachi one of the places in Pakistan that is most susceptible to army intervention. In 2011, ethno-political violence led to Karachi's business, trade, and industrial communities repeatedly calling for the army to declare a state of emergency and take control of security. Instead of intervening, the military pressured politicians to negotiate with militants.[51]

Karachi's uncontrolled urban sprawl also poses a significant security problem. The developments taking place in peripheral areas of the city are beyond the management capability of the government. *Katchi abadis*, or shantytowns, contain half of Karachi's population. These cramped slums have inadequate services; including sewage, water, and electricity, in addition to a lack of security.[52] The Karachi government's lenient policy towards housing regulation contributes to migration to the city from other parts of the country,[53] which further reduces governance capability and increases the outskirts of Karachi susceptible to the formation of an AGS.

Karachi's security situation has serious implications for U.S.-Pakistan relations because the megacity has emerged as a hub of militancy and terrorist attacks. The fundraising and recruitment of the TTP is a major element of the terrorist presence in Karachi, and as these groups consolidate power in the city, they could increase the current perception of Pakistan's ambivalence about fighting terrorism within its territory, further straining relations with the United States and encouraging intervention in the future.[54]

High-level interventions by the Pakistan Army and Supreme Court have helped to temporarily disrupt cycles of violence in Karachi. On March 11, 2015, Rangers raided the headquarters of the MQM party in Karachi, arresting 20 party members, seizing illegal weapons, and closing down the office. The United States and Amnesty International have accused the MQM and breakaway factions of human rights abuses, including torture and summary killings.[55] However, interventions such as the raid on MQM headquarters do not offer sustainable long-term solutions to Karachi's violent politics.

Lagos, Nigeria.

Although the United States imports 70 percent less oil from Nigeria than it did in 2003, in 2013, Nigeria still provided 3 percent of U.S. oil imports. That oil flows through Lagos, the commercial capital and deep-water port on the Gulf of Guinea. In addition to the port and its facilities, Lagos has a diverse economy with manufacturing and service industries, banking, telecommunications, and some more traditional activities including mining, agriculture, forestry, and fishing. It returns about 30 percent of Nigeria's gross domestic product and serves as the primary hub for international trade.[56]

Founded in 1472, Lagos was named by Portuguese explorers for its many lagoons, which cause a significant amount of its land area to be unsuitable for building or other infrastructure. In 1986, severe traffic congestion led to the relocation of Nigeria's political capital from Lagos to Abuja. Lagos' geography, while a source of valuable resources and infrastructure, is also one of its most problematic features, much like New York City. The DoD's *Megacities Report* profiled Lagos as:

> a loosely integrated megacity . . . composed of continuous urban sprawl primarily made up of buildings and informal structures of 1-3 stories, the majority of which are connected by informal dirt roads and large swaths of slums and shanties that are alternately governed. . . . Most of the slums float in the Lagos lagoon, and consist of shacks built to no construction standard. Yet, they have a school system, medical facilities, and even cell towers. Alternatively governed spaces will be more common in developing megacities in the future.[57]

Lagos officially became a megacity in 2010 and is one of the most densely populated cities in Africa. The population is estimated at 21 million, and it is the most populous metropolitan area in Nigeria as well as the second most populous and fastest-growing city in Africa after Cairo. Lagos currently ranks as the seventh fastest-growing city in the world, with 25 percent of all Africans being Nigerian.[58]

Since Nigeria returned to civilian leadership after civil war and multiple coups in 1999, the perception of corruption has declined steadily; however, due to increasing violence by the *Boko Haram* radical Islamic group and the response by the Nigerian Joint Task Force that frequently includes brutality against civilians, as well as ongoing environmental degradation and economic inequality, since the Fund for Peace began measuring state fragility in 2005, Nigeria has declined from 84.3 to 102.4, compared to the U.S. score for 2015 at 35.3.[59]

A series of reforms began in Nigeria in 1999 aimed at reducing inequality and increasing citizen participation in government at all levels. In Lagos, most citizens credit current Mayor Babatunde Fashola, often referred to as the "Mayor Bloomberg of Lagos State," for his high achievement in this area. Less visible signs of local government reform include improved basic service provision and physical infrastructure.

In June 2015, the World Bank's International Development Association granted a $200 million credit directly to the Lagos district government. These funds were intended to improve public finances to help maintain the state's recent economic growth and poverty reduction efforts and assist in continuing to provide social services. The World Bank noted that, "In the past decade Lagos State achieved significant economic growth, improved its infrastructure and services, significantly reduced crime, and brought millions of people out of poverty."[60]

Lagos State Government has also identified local stakeholder groups outside the elites with whom to implement more inclusive decision-making methods for economic and infrastructure development and planning. These include town hall meetings with local government officials to which groups from various districts are invited to participate, including market stallholders, landlords, community development representatives, and religious and traditional leaders. They are encouraged to openly and collaboratively discuss draft legislation and development plans before they are approved or implemented. Professor Michael Filani reports that:

> Traditional rulers serve as spokespersons for the community on issues such as granting lockup permits and tenement rates, and they are usually consulted to obtain their endorsement of other important issues. . . . [p]ublic expenditure by the local government is monitored by a statutory committee.[61]

Community groups are represented by both genders and even youths.

While positive strides have been made, Lagos' population density and the various islands that comprise it inherently create opportunities for subdivision easily subjected to alternative governance where the population is least served by the state and has the least economic opportunity or political power. As Nigeria is critical to maintaining stability in West Africa, and as Islamic terrorism continues to ravage the northern part of the country mainly in the form of *Boko Haram*, and as China's interest in Nigeria and its resources and logistical benefits increases, the country as a whole is of primary interest to U.S. military planners, with Lagos to become increasingly important in strategic thinking.

In northern Nigeria, recent violence has been perpetrated mainly by the Islamic militants *Boko Haram* and their offshoots. In the south, aside from criminal acts, violence is politically driven, not religious, and targets the wealth derived from the oil industry at the expense of the environment and lack of economic opportunity for those who live in the oil-rich areas. Although a peace was negotiated in 2009, some former associates of the violent Movement for the Emancipation for the Niger Delta (MEND) have resumed activities that include oil pipeline sabotage, kidnapping, and piracy in the Gulf of Guinea, as they do not feel the government has kept its side of the peace agreement by providing jobs and training opportunities for former MEND members.

Other types of political violence include the sort of post-election skirmishes that took place in northern Nigeria in April 2015. In Lagos, civil disturbance is often organized by local politicians who mobilize "Area Boys (and Girls)" for this purpose. Such activities do not constitute alternative governance, as these are isolated political activities and not structures controlling geographic areas. While the Nigerian Police Force (NPF) appears to be ubiquitous in urban areas, visiting U.S. officials are frequently asked to assist in the provision of community policing and law enforcement training, communications equipment, and vehicles to the NPF and local forces. This lack of resources, leadership, and training has led most Nigerians to doubt the NPF's effectiveness, to the extent that criminals operate with impunity, aside from local vigilante groups that occasionally capture perpetrators and kill them on the spot.[62]

In June 2013, the Lagos City Council announced that it had recruited 50 vigilantes to provide security from criminals who had been kidnapping and robbing local citizens, adding that the Council was so confident in this approach that it would be hiring even more for this purpose.[63] In January 2015, traditional leader Chief Moshood Balogun of Lagos' Idimuland announced a community-policing program in his area, which had local residents serving in a surveillance capacity combined with a vigilante group assisting the federal government. The program also calls for the purchase of new telecommunications equipment to help prevent incidents of sabotage and theft on the community's oil pipeline segments.[64]

Like the *Smotra* group in Moscow, as long as the vigilantes remain attuned to the specific tasks they have been mandated to conduct by the local authorities, this "community policing" might not burgeon into alternative governance; but a traditional chief employing local vigilantes to protect residents could also signal the opening salvo of the development of someplace like Idimuland as a separate geographical and political enclave moving further away from the host megacity and state. Monitoring such events is a significant task, but early warning will be the key to mission success in case of active missions to protect U.S. interests, such as maintaining an uninterrupted flow of Nigerian oil.

RECOMMENDATIONS

The subject of identifying the emergence of AGS and determining if they present a threat or opportunity to U.S. Army planners mirrors the enormity and complexity of megacities themselves, which would be impossible to treat comprehensively in this space. Directions for further breaking down the topic and addressing its critical aspects for additional study are the primary policy recommendations arising from this monograph.

Develop a Robust Alternative Governance Vulnerability Index.

As noted in the sections on dimensions of culture and measuring alternative governance, the metrics presented here are **only** a starting point for developing a predictive model that can be effectively tested and expanded to identify a fuller alternative governance vulnerability index. The metrics suggested here must be enhanced and combined with additional and varied information sources, including reliable HUMINT collection as expanded below. Then, each must be rigorously tested for validity and carefully weighted and applied to robust case studies augmented with field research. In this way, the Army can create a valuable indicator and warning model to identify the true social, political, and economic centers of gravity within megacities and their populations; detect any early shifts in these centers; determine the appropriate responses or monitoring; and finally define appropriate measures of mission success long before any considerations of force commitments are made. As Keister noted, "The challenges of seeing into such spaces also make it difficult to assign blame or locate and target those at fault in the event of undesirable outcomes — limiting America's ability to deter threatening activities."[65]

Intelligence Preparation of the Battlefield.

While the U.S. Army has always been good at geographic terrain analysis—augmented only in the past few decades by highly attuned reconnaissance tools such as aerial photography, satellites, and drones—these technological tools are of limited use in densely populated megacities with varying structural challenges. This makes the development of reliable HUMINT critical to developing solid indicators and warnings to trigger appropriate missions and define their success parameters.

In addition to HUMINT collection to identify power shifts, much like the effective use of native scouts in the Army's support of westward expansion, the use of local sources should be used to identify physical "turf" boundaries of emergent or nascent AGS and the degree of border solidity.

Finally, urban terrain analysis should be applied to megacities to determine whether natural or manmade geographic features inherently create boundaries between AGS. Identify whether the city layout, past and likely future growth patterns, or the natural terrain upon which it is located will inherently lend itself to alternative governance, or will it unless projected growth directions or controls are reconsidered.

Recognize the Growing Power of the Megacity Vis-à-Vis Surrounding States.

As megacities grow and states lose the ability to control them for various reasons, our view on their significance must increase as well. This was well noted in Richard Lamb's 2008 DoD study on ungoverned spaces and safe havens:

In many cases, provincial, local, tribal, or autonomous governments—and in some cases, other countries, corporations, or organizations—are simply better positioned than the central government to address the local conditions that enable illicit actors to operate there.[66]

Army intelligence elements could assist in the development of a robust HUMINT capability in megacities to begin clearly identifying the recruitment targets and understanding their social isolation or frustration with their current environment in order to infiltrate or partner with existing members of an AGS before conflicts require direct engagement. In the case of states that are failing to provide essential security and other services, the national military organizations and federal police are likely to be too well aware of the shortcomings, and members participating in U.S. military partnership activities such as joint training or the International Military Education and Training program, as well as National Guard pairings, are good starting points for developing effective indicator and warning information sources.

Identify and Enhance the Strength of "Civilizing Forces" within Megacities.

Across cultures and history, it is commonly women, religious leaders, and elders that exert the most influence in measures that reduce violence and enhance governance. Identifying centers of power under such leadership could be a signal of an AGS, active or nascent, with which the United States might align for enhanced governance across the megacity or state. This cooperation would be through "smart power" offensives, for which Army Civil Affairs might again partner with National Guard or State Department Foreign Affairs Officers for insights, as well as regional HUMINT experts.

ENDNOTES

1. Colonel Marc Harris *et al.*, "Megacities and the United States Army: Preparing for a Complex and Uncertain Future," Strategic Studies Group Report, Arlington, VA: Chief of Staff of the Army, Strategic Studies Group, June 2014, p. 3, available from *https://www.army.mil/e2/c/downloads/351235.pdf*, accessed on June 6, 2016.

2. Steven Pinker, *The Better Angels of Our Nature: Why Violence has Declined*, New York, NY: Viking, 2012, pp. 74-75.

3. Robert D. Kaplan, *The Revenge of Geography*, New York: Random House, 2012, pp. 121-122.

4. Jennifer Keister, "The Illusion of Chaos: Why Ungoverned Spaces Aren't Ungoverned, and Why That Matters," *Policy Analysis*, No. 766, December 9, 2014, Washington, DC: Cato Institute, p. 8.

5. *Ibid.*, p. 4.

6. Dr. Phil Williams updated his 2008 publication *From the New Middle Ages to a New Dark Age: The Decline of the State and U.S. Strategy*, Carlisle, PA: Strategic Studies Institute, U.S. Army War College; see Phil Williams, "Here Be Dragons: Dangerous Spaces and International Security," in Anne L. Clunan and Harold A. Trinkunas, eds., *Ungoverned Spaces: Alternatives to State Authority in an Era of Softened Sovereignty*, Stanford, CA: Stanford University Press, 2010.

7. Pinker, p. 106.

8. Sudhir Venkatesh, *Gang Leader for a Day: A Rogue Sociologist Takes to the Streets*, New York, NY: The Penguin Press, 2008, pp. 117-123.

9. "'GTA gang' kills drivers near Moscow, vigilantes on war-path after criminals," *Russia Times*, September 16, 2014, available from *www.rt.com/news/188152-gta-gang-manhunt-racers/*, accessed on August 15, 2015.

10. Interfax Information Services, "Moscow Police Official Brands Ethnic Gangs Main Problem," *Russia Beyond the Headlines*, November 7, 2014, available from *rbth.com/news/2014/11/07/moscow_police_official_brands_ethnic_gangs_main_problem_41209.html*, accessed on August 27, 2015.

11. *Ibid.*

12. William Reno, "Persistent Insurgencies and Warlords," in Clunan and Trinkunas, *Ungoverned Spaces*, p. 70.

13. Keister, p. 6.

14. James C. Scott, *Comparative Political Corruption*, Englewood Cliffs, NJ: Prentice-Hall, 1972, pp. 10-13; Joseph Lapalombara, "Structural and Institutional Aspects of Corruption," *Social Research*, Vol. 61, Iss. 2, 1994, p. 329.

15. German journalist Jürgen Todenhöfer on CNN's *Fareed Zakaria Global Public Square* special broadcast "Blindsided: How ISIS Shook the World," aired July 5, 2015 in the United States.

16. *Ibid.*

17. Geert Hofstede, *Cultures and Organizations: Software of the Mind*, New York: McGraw-Hill USA, 1997, p. 28.

18. Bryan W. Husted, "Wealth, Culture, and Corruption," *Journal of International Business Studies*, Vol. 30, Iss. 2, 2nd Qtr. 1999, pp. 339-360.

19. Pinker, pp. 74-75.

20. Rob Johnston, *Analytic Culture in the US Intelligence Community: An Ethnographic Study*, Washington, DC: Central Intelligence Agency, Center for the Study of Intelligence, 2005, p. 93.

21. *Ibid.*, p. 95.

22. M.S. Alam, "A Theory of Limits on Corruption and Some Applications," *Kyklos*, Vol. 48, 1995, p. 422.

23. Salim Rashid, "Public Utilities in Egalitarian LDC's: The Role of Bribery in Achieving Pareto Efficiency," *Kyklos*, Vol. 34, 1981, pp. 448-460.

24. Interview conducted by the author with Dr. David Overare in Erie, PA on August 28, 2015.

25. Transcript of CNN's Special Report, "Blindsided: How ISIS Shook the World," originally aired May 11, 2015, available from *www.cnn.com/TRANSCRIPTS/1505/11/csr.01.html*, accessed on July 20, 2015.

26. *Ibid.*

27. Harris *et al.*, p. 2.

28. *Ibid.*

29. *Ibid.*

30. Keister, p. 3.

31. Pinker.

32. Williams, "Here Be Dragons."

33. Pinker, p. 90.

34. Pinker, p. xxi.

35. Office of the United States Trade Representative Internet Resource Center on Nigeria, last update May 1, 2014, available from *ustr.gov/countries-regions/africa/west-africa/nigeria*, accessed on July 3, 2015.

36. See the annually produced "Corruption Perceptions Index," Transparency International, available from *www.transparency.org/research/cpi/overview*, accessed on June 16, 2016.

37. J. J. Messner *et al.*, "Fragile States Index: 2015," 11th annual ed., Washington, DC: *Foreign Policy Magazine*, for the The Fund for Peace, released on June 17, 2015, available from *fsi.fundfor-peace.org/*, accessed on July 3, 2015.

38. Shemrez Nauman Afzal, "Stabilizing Karachi," posted October 15, 2013, available from *spyeyesnews.blogspot.com/2013/10/stabilizing-karachi.html*, accessed on June 16, 2016.

39. Khawaja Amer, "Population explosion: Put an embargo on industrialisation in Karachi," *The Express Tribune*, October 6, 2013, available from *tribune.com.pk/story/614409/population-explosion-put-an-embargo-on-industrialisation-in-karachi/*, accessed on May 4, 2015; Huma Yusuf, "Conflict Dynamics in Karachi," *Peaceworks Report No. 82*, Washington: DC, U.S. Institute for Peace, October 2012, available from *spearheadresearch.org/SR_CMS/wp-content/up-loads/2012/11/Peace-Works-report-on-Karachi.pdf*, accessed on April 27, 2015.

40. Messner *et al.*, "Fragile States Index: 2014," 10th annual ed., Washington, DC: *Foreign Policy Magazine*, for the The Fund for Peace, released on June 24, 2014, available from *library.fundfor-peace.org/cfsir1423*, accessed on June 16, 2015.

41. Yusuf, "Conflict Dynamics in Karachi."

42. Huma Yusuf, "The Other Threat to Pakistan," *The New York Times*, April 2, 2014, available from *www.nytimes.com/2014/04/03/opinion/the-other-threat-to-pakistan.html*, accessed on May 2, 2015; Afzal.

43. *Ibid.*

44. *Ibid.*

45. Zia ur-Rehman and Declan Walsh, "Killings Rise in Karachi as Taliban Target Police," *The New York Times*, August 11, 2014, available from *www.nytimes.com/2014/08/12/world/asia/killings-rise-in-karachi-as-taliban-target-police.html*, accessed on May 1, 2015.

46. Faraz Khan, "Where law enforcers fear to tread: The entry fee for these spots of Karachi may be your life," *The Express Tribune*, March 23, 2013, available from *tribune.com.pk/story/525035/where-law-enforcers-fear-to-tread-the-entry-fee-for-these-spots-of-karachi-may-be-your-life-karachi-city/*, accessed on May 2, 2015.

47. Khan.

48. Yusuf, "Conflict Dynamics in Karachi."

49. Khan.

50. Afzal.

51. Yusuf, "Conflict Dynamics in Karachi."

52. Hina Mahgul Rind, "Katchi Abadis house half of Karachi's population," *The News International*, November 15, 2013.

53. Farhan Anwar, "Urban sprawl: Rethinking the management of Karachi's slums," *The Express Tribune*, November 25, 2013, available from *tribune.com.pk/story/636541/urban-sprawl-rethinking-the-management-of-karachis-slums/*, accessed on June 17, 2016.

54. Yusuf, "Conflict Dynamics in Karachi."

55. Aditya Tejas, "Pakistan Rangers Raid Karachi Offices Of Controversial Political Party MQM, Killing One," *International Business Times*, March 11, 2015, available from *www.ibtimes.com/pakistan-rangers-raid-karachi-offices-controversial-political-party-mqm-killing-one-1843138*, accessed on May 1, 2015.

56. Michael O. Filani, "The Changing Face of Lagos: from Vision to Reform and Transformation," Report funded by Foundation for Development and Environmental Initiatives (Nigeria), and Cities Alliance, September 2012, available from *www.citiesalliance.org/sites/citiesalliance.org/files/Lagos-reform-report-lowres.pdf*, accessed on August 10, 2015.

57. Harris *et al.*, p. 19.

58. "Lagos Population 2015," World Population Review website, available from *worldpopulationreview.com/world-cities/lagos-population/*, accessed on April 23, 2015.

59. Messner *et al.*, "Fragile States Index: 2015."

60. "World Bank Approves US$200 Million to Improve Public Finance and Investment Climate in Lagos," Press Release, The World Bank International Development Association, June 26, 2015, available from *www.worldbank.org/en/news/press-release/2015/06/26/world-bank-approves-us200-million-to-improve-public-finance-and-investment-climate-in-lagos*, accessed on August 5, 2015.

61. Filani.

62. "Nigeria 2014 Crime and Safety Report: Lagos," Overseas Security Advisory Council, Bureau of Diplomatic Security, Crime and Safety Report on Nigeria, Washington, DC: U.S. Department of State, available from *www.osac.gov/pages/ContentReportDetails.aspx?cid=15799*, accessed on August 3, 2015.

63. News Agency of Nigeria, "Insecurity: Lagos council employs 50 vigilantes to fight crime," *Premium Times*, June 28, 2013, available from *www.premiumtimesng.com/regional/ssouth-west/139806-insecurity-lagos-council-employs-50-vigilantes-to-fight-crime.html*, accessed on May 4, 2015.

64. News Agency of Nigeria, "Lagos Community Inaugurates Pipeline Vandalism Vigilante Group," *Leadership*, January 13, 2015, available from *leadership.ng/news/401567/lagos-community-inaugurates-pipeline-vandalism-vigilante-group*, accessed on May 2, 2015.

65. Keister, p. 6.

66. Dr. Robert Lamb, *Ungoverned Areas and Threats from Safe Havens*, Final Report of the Ungoverned Areas Project, Prepared for the Office of the Undersecretary of Defense for Policy, Washington, DC: Office of the Deputy Assistant Secretary of Defense for Policy Planning, 2008, available from *www.dtic.mil/get-tr-doc/pdf?AD=ADA479805*, accessed on May 4, 2015.

U.S. ARMY WAR COLLEGE

Major General William E. Rapp
Commandant

*****

STRATEGIC STUDIES INSTITUTE
and
U.S. ARMY WAR COLLEGE PRESS

Director
Professor Douglas C. Lovelace, Jr.

Director of Research
Dr. Steven K. Metz

Author
Ms. Diane E. Chido

Editor for Production
Dr. James G. Pierce

Publications Assistant
Ms. Denise J. Kersting

*****

Composition
Mrs. Jennifer E. Nevil